I0456349

FIRSTMATTERPRESS

Portland, Ore.

greenhouse

greenhouse

sophie hall

FIRSTMATTERPRESS

Portland, Ore.

Copyright © 2024 by Sophie Hall
All rights reserved

First Edition

Published in the United States
by First Matter Press
Portland, Oregon

Paperback ISBN-13: 978-1-958600-09-2
Library of Congress Control Number: 2024940632

This project was funded in part by the
Literary Arts Oregon Literary Fellowship
for Publishers. literary-arts.org

Editor: ash good
Contributing Editors: Lauren Paredes, Hailey Spencer & Emily Moon
In Cohort: Clara McAuley
Contributing Readers: Sonya Wohletz & Riley Danvers
Copy Editor: Andra Vltavín

Cover: *Green House*
18.25 inches x 27.5 inches (flashe, acrylic, and oil on paper)
Copyright © 2024 by Alexandra Strenfel
alexandrastrenfel.com

Book design by ash good
ashgood.com

For all I've tried my best to keep alive,
and for all who've kept me.

Contents

Home

I am most at home in what is ugly.

I grew up in a house unfit for public display. Walls I drew on as a child were never painted over. Scribbles aged like fine art.

When something broke, it was fixed with what was easy or not at all. Cracked windows were boarded up and disguised with strategically placed blankets. Decomposing bathroom tiles were obscured from view with a stool. The dryer worked irregularly. My father hung a clothesline for the months our breath made little clouds indoors: yellow rope laced the hallway, damp turtlenecks and jeans dripping rivers between floorboards.

When the bathroom sink stopped working, we moved our toothbrushes to the kitchen without comment. Mint blobs dotted dirty dishes like molded cherries on top of half-eaten desserts.

A dim house greeted me often, courtesy of overdue electric bills. We developed routines. In winter, I carried frozen pizzas outside and packed them in snow. I washed my hair with bottled Deer Park water and put on mascara by flashlight glow and wore the same skinny jeans to school for days, classmates none the wiser.

I folded paper fans for summer heat. My sister copied me. My brother built a generator out of a lawnmower that powered a third of the house. Extension cords weaved around the furniture, holding our pieces together.

Mr. Yuk's stuck-out tongue stickered boarded windows. We scoured cushions for loose quarters to buy white bread at the Liberty station. I wore mock necks from flea markets, daisy-print gingham dug from haphazard Goodwill aisles.

My family bonded on Walmart excursions funded by food stamps. I swam in a pool fashioned from a felled satellite dish, painted green. We turned trips to the convenience store down the road into expeditions, routed through the oaks behind the house. I bit into a Hershey's bar after the long walk as if its melted milk chocolate was my first hot meal after months in cold.

Sunlight glittered through the translucent front porch roof in patterns that mimicked swimming chlorophyll. The green my mother painted chipped and flailed off the sides of the house, blending with uncut grass.

I tore the grass up with my hands—for my stuffed animals and dolls, making salad.

Everyone Revolved

I saw red where the green porch chipped. Colors shrink-wrapped in snow, pizza and cereal boxes deflated and affixed to floorboards like door mats. The back porch once had center steps. Once, it was an open space, with a path that led down to a picnic table in the quiet grasp of a gazebo.

He closed the back porch in. Wood board upon wood board upon wood board, planks the same size as those he used to build coffee tables and gun safes. Turned bare railing into walls, eliminated the steps. He probably justified it by the rotting planks beneath our feet. Turned green once red to brown. When he stopped, it would stand still: half raw wood, half stained.

He froze the gazebo the same way. Clothed it in leftovers from an odd construction job mixed with pieces of our own receding backyard woods. It became a shed layered with gray shingles. He told my sister and me that it would be our playhouse. It became storage for thin cardboard boxes of Coke and RC cans, our sustenance the weight inside a glacier.

The half-houses my father built became homes of the pets we didn't let in. Little paws padded into the sheltered cold. Woke up baby blue. Didn't wake up.

We didn't know the kittens were coming. Generations formed in bellies like seam-ripped baseballs, most of them born from one cat he bestowed with the name Fastball. I imagine her wandering over as a kitten from the neighbor's house into the backyard my father mowed in the shape of a baseball diamond. He'd toss the pitch above her head for it to whiz towards the acorn-fruiting oaks beyond, no arms reaching for it.

Fastball was the only one of his baseball names that stuck. Her legacy lived on in little leagues, charcoal kittens and snow kittens and kicked-dust kittens and mixes of everything. Fastball survived litters that ran into semi-trucks and vanished into the woods and never opened their eyes. Fastball churned out kittens with flattened faces that lasted a week in our world, attempts at reincarnation for her children lost to the road. They followed her with pupils that looked in different directions, anywhere but at what was right in front of them.

They ran into the house when the screen door swung open with thin gusts of wind. My allergies flared, and I confused the cause: black cat fur, black mold. Kittens perched on the triangle steps at one part of the back porch that didn't get closed in and waited there until I walked outside at four in the morning, a middle-school insomniac. I watched the sun rise with their paws on my socks. They jumped off and wagged their tails like shark fins through the weeds that would swallow my waist if I walked any further. The sea of weeds grew from a hole my father made to fill with water. He didn't finish that pond, months later returning the same dirt to it strewn with crushed plastic hamburger buns and Polly Pocket cars.

Dogs incessantly scratched their necks. Dwarf hamsters escaped into the walls. Mice crawled on the top shelf of my closet and dropped to my dresser drawers. Still awake, I wondered if I'd met them before.

We held hunted salamanders in mittened hands before setting them free in the front yard pond, the first one our father had made years before, the one that held its ground. We adorned plastic cages with sea-glass pebbles and fringed ferns. We made them beautiful homes. Then we forgot. The screen door slammed shut. Their eyes and spines shriveled in the afternoon sun.

My father moved red-bellied snake after red-bellied snake from the yard to the terrariums on top of the television stand, where he could watch below them until he fell asleep. He named them all Copernicus, after Doc's dog in *Back to the Future*.

A pet-store mouse's black belly grew golf balls after a few days in our home. I woke to the sounds of a children's choir buried in wood chips.

I watched the sun rise, nocturnal. Rays illuminated a yellow Croc my sister once lost outside, the age when she lost it impossible to tell since its size had warped with the sun.

My father dug a pond, and dug a pond, and dug another pond.

Goldfish stiffened in winter and shook off the pause the next season.

Fastball got inside and shredded my One Direction posters into bedding in closet corners, preparing for the next generation she'd try to keep alive.

It Takes a Community To Make a Candle

How do you capture the spirit of a memory in a way that feels personal and recognizable to everyone?

West Virginia Candle

Recall afternoons in the Mountain State. The scents of honeysuckle, baked cookies, and sweet bourbon mix with rich maple syrup and musk.

What do I make from the rest?

FIRST BEDROOM,
FIRST BATHROOM

RATING ★ ★ ★

Honey, cinnamon, and faint strawberry reconstruct the few feet
between your childhood bedroom and the bathroom across the hall.
Homemade facial masks rot in Mason jars under your bed. Imagined
elegance sparkles in bottles of carbonated water. This scent rewinds
age in all ways except looks.

> *Top Notes: From-a-bear-jar honey, mixed-with-sugar cinnamon,
> artificial strawberry*
>
> *Mid Notes: Baking soda, lemon, nutmeg*
>
> *Base Notes: Solutions to your acne found in the spice cabinet, a
> mascara-flecked bathroom mirror, the ink-dreg image of Lana
> Del Rey printed on 8.5 x 11 paper peeling off your wall, domestic
> imperfections you try to blur out*

**TYPICAL BURN TIME IS 24–48 HOURS BUT DEPENDS ON
HOW PERTINENT DAYDREAM IS TO SURVIVAL**

REVIEW: You will miss these times, occasionally. You'll miss them most
when life feels stable. When you grow up and find yourself unable to
breathe, cat-hair allergy turning wet concrete in your lungs, you will sip
tea that testifies to the improvement of respiratory wellness. Healthy
portions of licorice and mint—flavors you never liked. You'll add honey

and mix it into water before adding the tea bag. For a second, it will take you back to ninth grade: every night sticky with kitchen-mixed facial masks, honey coating the edges of your fingertips and the hair above your ears, your skin stiff all over as it dried.

Before your tea mug came the old house's bathtub—ceramic with warmth just barely lingering as the clock shifted to one in the morning instead of that faraway, adult eight o'clock. You used to sit in that water like it made you softer, like Juno Temple in the intro of *Little Birds*—away from the world and yet directly inside the most concrete parts of yours—imagining a more grown-up and refined nostalgia, a romanticized clawfoot bubble-bath version of eventual loss.

*

Heart Notes: What am I hiding?

Facial Mask or Pancake Mix or Something Else: I am so focused on hiding the finished jars of homemade facial masks under my bed that I forget about the bowls I use to mix them. One morning, Dad's voice echoes from the bathroom with my name: *Is this your pancake mix on the shelf?* I cannot own up to the concoction being mine. It's the same embarrassment when my brother knocks on the bathroom door in the middle of the night because he has to pee and I hurriedly drain the bathwater to not look like such a weirdo, orange peels and tea bags floating, my face slimed with honey. Or when my sister finds love letters to imagined muses in a journal I've accidentally left somewhere in the open.

Matches

On the bleachers, there are plates
labeled with my brother's, sister's, and my name
(gifts from our

father). His arm hair knotting
around my sister, skinny
in her basketball shorts.

Her arms are so thin, almost
matchsticks.

Our father used to build us houses,
six-inches, stacked from matchsticks
in our sister-shared bedroom—our childhood
dusting ash over his constructions:

little houses we could see into
and one singed cage.

How she's shrunk to fit
that old uniform, what's rekindled—
his wooden arms

oak-trunk wooden, gun-cabinet wooden
sanding-baseball-bats-in-the-backyard wooden.

She carries splinters with her
decorative plate, a reward at the end of the game.

I sit in sawdust on the bleachers
with the other gifts, our left-behind names
spelled in burnt matches
across empty plates.

My sister, a stick
striking old stubble.

Home Movie

I'm going to miss you when you go.
—Ron Franz, *Into the Wild*

It seemed like everything became centered and peaceful
when there was no choice but to make nature the focus.
—Carine McCandless, *The Wild Truth: A Memoir*

> September 22, 2020
> 3:03 PM
> Voice Mailbox
> Highway noise rumbles before gravel shoots up.
> *Sophie! How you doin hey this is your dad. I'm on my*
> *way home from work. Just givin you a call to make*
> *sure you got my new number.*

*

In the foggy age of early middle school, I journey to Alaska through
a bulky television screen, trapezoid-shaped with heft hidden by the
stand's frail wood frame. I am sitting on a clammy leather couch
with clean socks strewn over and under my lap. Eddie Vedder plays
behind shots of open roads and evergreen pines far taller than I have
ever seen. Parents suggest a new car for a son who responds that his
Datsun runs fine. *Things, things, things*, he spits out in detest. There
isn't a clear image of my father's first encounter with this phrase, but I
see him testing it. Mentally or verbally. He probably guffaws and slaps
his knee, shouts it, knocks a few VHS tapes off the coffee table. He is
going to use it later.

We pick black raspberries in mid-July, multicolored acorns on the odd year. We salamander hunt from spring to the last drops of September. Silky brown ones usually rest under decaying logs. Giant ones with white spots on inky skin can be found underneath heavy rocks—to our small hands and kicking feet, their homes are boulders. When we flail, our father moves the rocks aside with all the strength and skill in the world.

The best hunts turn up babies, pinky-fingernail-sized, curled up and mistaken for millipedes. Sometimes we think we've caught the smallest newborn only to find that it's the cutoff tail of an adult, ejected to fool its predator.

We snatch them with hands wrapped in Ziploc bags, plunk their striped and spotted bodies in containers with air holes drilled in the lid as if it is possible to counter the overwhelming stench of our father's coffee grounds. We take them back up to the house and set our catches free to zig-zag across the front yard pond, but the babies, or the Godzillas, we keep like trophies in dollar-store terrariums, staring at their vast differences in innocence and size until we have to go inside.

*

When Chris finds the abandoned bus that will become his home, he stands on its roof and yells into Alaska's stretches of sun-blinding white: *IS THERE ANYBOOOODY HEEEEERE?* The echo of his own voice greets him, the smile in it slicing through the cold.

We go to the woods under the guidance of our father. Usually. My sister and I poke and prod his sleeping shoulders until he yells to go away or gives into our wishes. Other times, he is already stalking the woods himself.

We stand on top of Big Rock at the entrance, shouting his name into foxglove towers until he howls back from the belly of the woods. When he doesn't, neighbors bellow, *I'M NOT YOUR DADDY*, a reverberation that reawakens a familiar shame. My sister and I take up silence, and therefore solitude, for weeks. On other days, he exits only for us to immediately pull him back in. Sometimes, he refuses. We look at each other, follow his back to the green house we'd just left, sulking. Sometimes, we sink between the weaving oaks anyway.

One day, I take my bike alone. Pedal over bumps and down the main trail. I pick up speed and overpower all roots in my path with my chin raised high. But as I keep on, my eyes water, and I push my head down until I am tangled in handlebars and dirt and fern spores. Overhead leaves mix and spin. My lungs hang dry and heavy.

I hear footsteps.

Are you okay? My sister pulls me from the ground. I lean on her uphill until our half-red porch peeks through the black raspberry bushes and we gather our strength to sprint over our dandelion-spotted backyard baseball field.

Inside, I keep a backpack under my bed. When parents fight, I add a book, a journal, a bag of Doritos, or my most-recently discovered pocket change. It will support my mother and siblings in the cover of the forest, or just me. Every so often, when the kitchen gets low, I take out whatever previously stashed snack the bag contains but make a note to replenish when the groceries get restocked.

*

January 15, 2021
Sometime in the morning
Missed Call: I am working and don't pick up.

*

Sometime after the divorce (after fifth grade), Dad brings home a DVD. He does this. He's the truest companion to the five-dollar bin, the highlight of any Walmart trip. This DVD has a rusting, half-green bus on the cover. A young man sits on top, his mullet windblown. A few branches are visible through the front window of the frozen bus—Chris, with his spoon poised at the edge of a just-cracked-open can of beans, is the only thing that suggests movement. *Into the Wild.* I don't remember the first time I watch it, but I remember how often, after this, I want to. We sit on the couch together, alone, watching Chris cut up his credit cards and donate piles of money. Everything. Every time, Dad repeats his words about *things*. Money. His cackle echoes as I peel the thick outer skin off a Monster Slim Jim with my teeth.

Sometimes, when we spend all the food stamps in one trip or ask for something before learning not to, he falls back on Chris. He runs his hands through his hair until it sticks up with grease and scorns *things, things, things*. He talks about leaving, our way to get out of here, or maybe just his. We are silent as he goes on, louder and louder, but we still listen. Hope.

When we get home after a tense car ride, he puts the movie in the player and heads to the basement to stack logs and cereal boxes in the furnace. When he keeps us warm this way, the walls smell like birthday candles or campfire. Every so often, the wood burner's clanging metal door coincides with the acoustic soundtrack. Chris recites Sharon Olds' "I Go Back to May 1937" to his sister, and she asks, *Who wrote that?* He says, *It could've been either one of us, couldn't it?*

My sister watches with me for a little while. My brother storms immediately to his room with the marked punctuation of cowboy boots. I sit in silence until our father comes back up, sprinkled with ash. He ruffles through his crumpled coat pockets where they lay atop the gun cabinet. Something jingles, the sound of nickels or keys.

One time, he pulls the DVD out at the end credits and hands it to me. *Keep it in your room*, he winks.

Into the Wild begins with a letter, yellow words across the TV screen: *I am prepared and have stocked all necessary comforts to live off the land for a few months.*

In the weeks following our mother's departure, my sister claims her old bedroom. We no longer have to share. Our father remains where he's always been, sleeping on the couch—out in the open.

For so long, what we know of the living room past bedtime is the sound of our parents clashing. Where our father sleeps, banished from the bedroom, they fight. One night, all three of us kids curl up in my brother's bedroom, in the center between the two others— when my mother opens the door and what has been faceless floods inside. *You kids have heard him—tell him—he's never wanted us anyway. He always says he'd rather live out in the woods on his own. Tell him.* And somehow the door closes, and the sound continues, or it stops.

When all three of us kids stay up all night in our own bedrooms, I will wonder if this is why he disappears into the basement, making up tales of the Sump Pump monster that haunts the space beyond the wood burner he stuffs full, warning us away. Or the woods, where Bigfoot roams and black bears carve warnings into the oaks that match the cuts of his pocket knife.

*

Summers, the house is hot and dead. I pass through the living room to fabric sopping from the ceiling fan. Sunlight floods our center window and filters through pant legs. My father's unconscious breath lifts the far frays of his cutoff denim shorts.

This place is so *full*, even on the occasion that the center of the room is clean, the floor swept of stray nuts and bolts and cinnamon toast dust. Between wooden floorboards, on top of wooden cabinets, on the TV stand and cluttered around each piece of furniture swarms an abundance of everything and nothing. Stamped envelopes—bills—that won't be opened, laundry that will take days to sort which bedroom it belongs to. Caps and coats with stuffed pockets and emerald guitar picks that sometimes stick to the black heels of my socks.

Dad's various girlfriends take it upon themselves to make our home fit for company, but eventually they all resort to the same methods we do, stuffing the junk and wire and unending cutoff cigarette filters and clothing scraps into cabinets, sweeping it under couches, unseen. The place is meant to be rough around the edges.

I pass through the living room and retreat to the woods with my sister. When it looks bleakest, we ride our bikes. In later years, we go beyond the trails where we gathered acorns as children to worlds unknown. Where we can still pick bleeding berries but from bushes we haven't tasted before. We trudge on until we reach the creek that usually marks the end of our exploration with our father. Unsupervised, we drop our bikes to the crabapple-littered ground and enter.

My sneakers sink in the water but float ever so slightly, shielding my skin from poking rocks. My sister steps ahead of me and then slips behind. We alternate, one leading and then the other. She checks the depth of the flood with a stick while I fill my pockets with snowflake-black and sandpaper rocks.

We talk about school, and West Virginia, and leaving Mount Storm. We talk about everyone who doesn't like us. Sometimes I say things she doesn't know how to respond to. The latest homophobic stabs from my classmates. My unaddressed identities fall into the water beneath us, runt crabapples with soundless weight. I don't know how to come out to her except in the way others frame me. But sometimes she's the one talking, and I don't know what to say. Brief conversation about her boyfriends who whisper slurs in the hallway.

We go until the world is golden. We make the trek a number of times, but every time, at the end, a green hill rises, some sunlit, chlorophylled cousin of our house in the opposite direction. We perch precariously on stream stones and boulders until water turns to grass and we climb up to the fields we usually only pass in cars, looking out at cows and hay bales in the distance. Only then do we turn back.

*

> January 15, 2021
> Sometime in the evening
> I do pick up: *Hello, hello, hello*
> to silence, and silence, and silence.

*

I retreat to my bedroom with the seasons. I stay up all night talking to online friends in messages that glow on the computer screen. One, homeschooled, from Bowling Green, Kentucky, longs for public school. I long for one in a *real city* full of people I don't and will never know the middle names of. From virus-riddled websites, we watch movies about escape: *Little Birds*, *Eternal Sunshine of the Spotless Mind*, *Wristcutters*. We press play on *Into the Wild* at the same time. We make plans to run away. I will pack whatever food won't go bad and sleep on ferns and feast on wild berries until I am anywhere but here.

Other times I watch *Into the Wild* on my own. If the internet has been shut off, I tramp to the garage to bring out a blocky yard-sale television, which I will keep as a private theater for a few weeks or months before deciding to rearrange my bedroom. I get a DVD player from the cabinet we keep full of them—stowaways beneath the living room television set, behind stained-box VHS tapes stacked in skyscrapers that hide the furniture. Unearthing the machine, plastic clatters and worn cardboard covers collide with one another, muffled.

On the top bunk, I chew stale hot-wing-flavored Ruffles and skinny long Slim Jims past the expiration date. I think to myself, *As soon as I can drive, I'll leave.* The Datsun floods on screen. Chris sets fire to crumpled dollar bills, and I imagine what will burn as I flee.

*

A chill seeps into walls. Snow buries roads and piles the front door. School gets canceled for weeks. I stay up all night, watching. Chris renames himself, writing with trash-can lipstick on a public bathroom mirror: *Alexander Supertramp.* The soundtrack brings in a flute. I pull sketchbooks from under the bed and spread them over floorboards, glitter and crackle nail polish aging in the cracks. Flip pages, rip them out. Charcoal and acrylic layer my nails until their weight falls on everything I touch.

Outside melts.

Sunlight shines through Mountain Lightning bottles. We come home from school and interrogate our father on the state of our migration. *When are we moving?* The question has become our lifeline in the years we've spent alone with him in the house, since the day our mother picked us up from school and carried us towns away with the clothes and hamster cages in the car, only for that escape to be twisted as kidnapping, for us children to be renamed pawns in a war.

When are we moving? He raises his eyebrows and says, *Soon, definitively.* With a chuckle. Other times, he offers nothing or something, loudly. Despite a lack of progress, I carry his promise with me, telling myself in his voice that we will all escape soon enough. That it will happen in one swift movement, the same way he'll randomly reveal a Sacagawea gold dollar from his smoky coat pocket. The few dollars to his name, he exchanges paper for gold, as if a flashy reveal makes them worth more.

The kitchen stagnates.

Someone asks if the food stamps have come yet. No one keeps track except me—always on the third, except Sundays. Some of those Sundays we're in Mom's warm house, so we don't feel the emptiness. Her pantry is reliable with goldfish crackers, tomato sauce, and marshmallow fluff. I wonder what my father feels, alone and roads away, while I'm slathering the stuff on graham crackers in her soft-lit kitchen. I go for straight spoonfuls, swallowing big gulps of guilt.

The third takes us to Walmart, late-night. We walk out with a receipt that trails the ground and three carts full of boxed and bagged things to dwindle over the next month, the food card hollow in Dad's hands. In the driver's seat, his hair sticks up, and shame turns to rant against all the *things* in the world that have harmed us, him. *Your mother—the government—your mother's new man—they*—us—it sludges in my pinky-stuffed ears, grease. My head rattles against the icy window. When we get home, I bring *Into the Wild* out from my bedroom, and we watch in silence until *things, things, things* bring crying laughter.

*

January 15, 2021
Sometime later in the evening
I am brave enough to text: *You called?*

*

School lets out. Without weekday school hours as a buffer, my brother's prized lawnmower-generator can't bear the weight of everything.

June amplifies our reliance on one another. I trade the toaster, my brother's finished jelly-spread lunch, for three minutes of my hair straightener. Smooth my cowlicks before throwing them in a ponytail. Without power, we have no screen-lit escapes, not even the light behind Chris's face. My sister and I stand in the front yard for thirty minutes and contemplate walking to the park, where we rarely go. We pace. *Just do it*, she says. I hesitate. *Go now*, I say. We are always daring each other to do something we will ultimately do together. We set off in the opposite direction of the gas station, taking the gravel strip beside the road.

Uphill for ages and then downhill for a little—everything stutters, rocky. Fields that take seconds in the car take hours to pass on foot, and the day's trailed-off sunlight still presses down on our shoulders, the air like the sweaty grip of Play-Doh, something not quite defined. Unidentifiable roadkill litters the road. A car honks, but neither of us can see a face through the windows: it is too bright, and the path so small that we walk single file. I move to grass so I can walk without fear of being driven into, my body scraped across little stones.

We turn back at the water tower, a third of the way. Run to the other side of the road so we face cars and can see all the loud things barreling towards us. Downhill and uphill, bumpy. Dull, shaded by maples. A deer carcass interrupts our adventure with flies and maggots. We veer into the darkening woods until it fades out of sight, but I still cannot swallow correctly the whole way home.

*

January 16, 2021
7:18 AM
*Yeah but figured you were busy with school
so then texted, and there is no mention of the silence
or the hellos or anything else at all.*

*

The abandoned Datsun is found and identified. In the voice of his sister, the movie tells us: *There were no signs that Chris had intended to return to it, but there wasn't any evidence of struggle, either. The police thought that Chris had chosen to leave it behind, and not that it was taken from him.*

For two years, everything I write references salamanders captured by children's hands. Backyard pet cemeteries. A map told in tree trunks. Grease. My father's face blurs.

But before that, we do move. I can't tell you how it happens. Dad would say, *It'll all work out.* For years, he said it, and though most of the time we stayed stuck in place, it felt comforting to hear him say it, a myth I wanted to be true. But the last summer without electricity is the last. His new girlfriend donates half our lives to Goodwill, including his purple pants. His new girlfriend won't leave my brother, who isn't coming, with the toaster. None of it is simple, but it happens, and I spend my last two years of high school in a Western Washington town.

Senior year, I share a bedroom with my fifteen-year-old sister. One night, my father watches a movie in the living room. It finishes as I pass through the kitchen. He suggests that I pop in *Into the Wild.* The DVD isn't there, but we find it online. That's something we can do now.

It starts. Chris becomes disillusioned, argues with his parents, leaves.

My father leaves the room. A door shuts.

Chris renames himself, faces his fear of swimming with a sprint into the ocean, bites the burned body of a small animal, seeks contentment on his own. His estrangement from his parents hangs over his adventure and everyone he meets. The last person he spends time with, an old man named Ron, asks to adopt him. Chris asks if they can talk about it when he gets back from Alaska.

I finish it, alone.

I apply to private colleges on the east coast like I have something to prove. I'm the first to sixth period English every day. The teacher asks how my application to Wellesley is going. My financial aid isn't. I come home to ask my father to fill out tax forms, and he's quiet, then not. *You don't understand these things.* The words I'd taken to heart from Chris' true-story movie-mouth, from my father's mouth so many times before, spill out again—about sick *society*, the sourness of *things*, the confinement of *money*—and this time, I feel them like a rubber band that had been stretching out while I forgot it would either end up breaking or snapping back.

Later, I find a familiar DVD in a tight new Walmart wrapper on my bed. I slam it back on the kitchen counter. It disappears.

Later, his voice lowers. I weigh my future, passing it awkwardly from my hands to his. *It'll all work out.* A pat on my back in our skinny apartment kitchen. Chris enters his new, unattached home, the Alaskan wilderness, by crossing a winter stream. When things get hard—his hunted moose mangled by maggots before he can smoke it, his supplies dwindling in the magic bus—he packs up and attempts to return to the world he left behind. The stream rushes with spring's violent thaw. This nature he'd chosen, with an eager heart and little preparation, becomes his trap. Despite the knowledge he'd carried for years in his field guide, he confuses similar plants and swallows poison, dead in his sleeping bag in days.

It'll all work out. I imagine what's behind his words—some secret college fund, stability he's had waiting for this moment, something to protect me. I know the chances of these safety nets existing, but I believe him.

HONDA
CRV

RATING ★ ★ ★ ★

Not quite air freshener, not quite cigarette smoke, not sweet or clean but not totally to the point of bowling-alley carpet—this scent will take you back to that everyday familiar family car, as if your Converse are still gum-stuck to its floor.

> *Top Notes: Like-Lemonhead air freshener, sister's borrowed Bath-and-Body-Works hot-cocoa, yesterday's cigarette smoke*

> *Mid Notes: Spilled Coca Cola, spilled other things*

> *Base Notes: The book you are currently reading tucked close to your nose, your head leaning on the cold window to clear your sinuses, fast-food wrappers balled under the seat, pretending you are in any of the places flinging by*

TYPICAL BURN TIME IS THE 30 MINUTES IT TAKES TO GET TO ANOTHER TOWN, OR THE 1-3 HOURS IT TAKES TO GET ANYWHERE YOU WANT TO BE

REVIEW: You are always ready to go. You always have a book with you, probably one you have read thirty times, like Nancy Werlin's *Impossible* or David Yoo's *Stop Me If You've Heard This One Before* (both novels you received as Christmas gifts from someone who didn't know you very well but for some reason found the story you'd use to escape).

When your mother goes to the grocery store, so do you; when they divorce and your father gets the car, you're the one who motivates him to go shopping. Waking him from a deep slumber is instinct, and at that time of the month, you bring him the phone and the SNAP balance number. You've already got your shoes on. They stay on most of the day while he drifts in and out of sleep. He finally rumbles awake at six, seven, eight o'clock in the evening, sometimes kinetic and itching to put his hands on a steering wheel. Other times, he's exasperated, running his hands so furiously through his hair that his body expends all energy in a half hour and then knocks out again.

At his most animated, the drive is Rob Zombie and headbanging. His hands swerve the steering wheel erratically to mimic metal noise. He doesn't smoke in the car, but you can smell it on him. On a good day, he stops at Little Caesars for a Hot n' Ready. Your mouth waters over garlic crust in the half-hour drive. You quietly sneak pepperoni slices.

Other times, your nose stuffs up with the heat vent dust. Tires crunch ice below you, and the sound weasels through the one earbud that doesn't work. Sometimes there is so much snow the entire windshield turns white. All around you: white. You can see the smoke of his breath and yours. You wonder how he gets you home—and he always does—when the path ahead looks so aimless.

*

Where am I going?

Take Me Home, Country Roads: The school gymnasium
during any celebration that manages to smell spiced
and warm. Eighth grade graduation. End-of-the-year
attendance ceremonies. The Christmas Program,
religion in public school. John Denver brings us all
together in the lyrical version of when one of the
eighteen classmates I am with all day responds to
gossip with: *It's okay—we're all family here.*

Maple Festival: Mom sets up her jewelry booth, and by the end of the day, someone has stolen one of her necklaces from its severed-neck display, exposed plastic collarbone where the wire should hang. I quietly walk back and forth between her booth and the neighboring one, eyeing the old man's carved and painted wooden animals, bulldogs and horses, owls with bodies of separate glued portions. He gives me one for free. I charm my favorite seller at every one of these festivals.

I am first of my siblings to call the passenger seat of her loaded Honda CRV, jumping at the chance to leave town to festivals and markets for eight or twelve or forty-eight hours even when I nauseate at my re-reads beneath the market table, the same stories stickying my fingers. I curl on concrete and lean against the bubble-wrap tub, turning pages. Legs knock at the tablecloth, Mom's poised in flamingo stance, one eggshell-blue UGG boot flat against her other thigh.

In a quiet moment between sales, she leans down and offers me a maple-leaf-shaped cake of maple sugar. It crumbles down my clothes and leaves a permanent crust on the cover of *The Devil Wears Prada.*

The Apples Are Upside Down

how we rolled up the carpet so we could dance, and the days
were bright red, and every time we kissed there was another apple
—Richard Siken, "Scheherazade"

ON A FIRST DATE

She had me at: *I eat three apples a day*, and I didn't even care about
the fruit.

She liked Gala. It was one of the first things I learned about
my girlfriend, Mia, on our first date (Veteran's Day, 2019), as casual
as mentioning what either of us had eaten before meeting for hot
chocolate at 11th Hour in downtown Bellingham. Gala. A name with an
atmosphere of elegance. I dreamt about taking her out in a suit and
tie and bringing her apples instead of roses.

Mia wasn't red to me, or at least not candy apple. Something
softer. Blush. Rouged skin of golden crabapples, the kind that hit
autumn ground without bruising. Chartreuse and orange, first hint of
seasons changing. Caramel. Colors I began to think in the more I saw
her, the more shades of her sweaters I got to know.

She had me at: *They're roses—part of the same family.*

Why Do Sliced Apples Turn Brown?

To reduce browning in apples, keep the slices refrigerated
to slow the reaction. You can also coat them with lemon or
pineapple juice. The acids in these juices slow the reaction,
and the antioxidants inhibit it. If you don't mind the added
sugar, covering the slices with honey, caramel, or sugar
syrup effectively blocks their exposure to oxygen.

IN THE MOVIES

When Matt Damon gets the girl in *Good Will Hunting*, he spots a guy who'd pursued the same girl inside a nearby restaurant as he leaves the bar. Matt/Will knocks on the window and says, muffled: *Do you like apples?* The guy nods, irritated. Sure. Then Matt/Will slams the napkin with her digits on the transparent wall between them: *How do you like them apples?* My body has derived more building blocks from this line than it has gained from the fruit. Every apple I bite into, something stops me halfway through: browning of flesh activating picky eating habits, visible seed turning my teeth hyper-aware and sensitive, boredom.

It was easy to find the *Good Will Hunting* VHS with my small hands at the top of the pile of them in the living room of my childhood, its presence marked by a large baseball imprint in the nearby wall. Sometimes Will and I were alone. Other times, the background snore broke. A familiar series of sounds followed: sizzle and crack of spine, reignited snore and pause and bleary repetition, *How do you like them apples?* In my father's voice, *apples* were formed from cigarette smoke, unbrushed teeth, and months of oversleep. Will was another one of his movie-men, young geniuses who throw their old, sad lives away.

Chew the line long enough to get the taste out. Swallow. Matt's got the look of every boy I obsessed over as a preteen, like Ralph Macchio from the 1986 *Crossroads* or young Leo DiCaprio. It's a look soft enough for a girl to swoon over, but I looked for it in the mirror more than I did in boys at school.

Unwrapping the Terry's Chocolate Apple

The Terry's 'Dessert Chocolate Apple' was made from 1926 before being outshone by the Chocolate Orange, which eventually led to the halt in production of the apple in 1954.

Found amongst Terry's other beautifully illustrated
luxury chocolate boxes, [...] the Chocolate Apple (and the
Chocolate Orange) were once seen as special chocolates,
perhaps only eaten on special occasions or in the homes
of the 'better off'.

IN THE KITCHEN

Growing up, we didn't have apples in the kitchen. Sometimes we had
apple-flavored things. Green apple jolly ranchers. Apple juice. Apple-
filled toaster strudels, if whoever picked them out from Walmart
messed up, or had a change of taste from our usual raspberry, or
that's all that was left in the freezer aisle. Sometimes Dad might
come home with one and break it into clean slices, the same way
those pre-divided chocolate oranges from our tattered Christmas
stockings, in the years Mom still put them up, required a hard tap
for the segments to simultaneously fracture. *This is the good stuff.*
This is how you know it's good. Never mind that he wasn't ever really
saying what *this* was.

He used the same language when smashing black raspberries
from the woods into a glass of milk, adding sugar. Procuring fruit,
rarity: store-bought blackberries delicate in his grip, kiwi soft like his
stubble. Like his hands weren't usually buried in polypropylene bags
of Lay's. The dietary change was exclusive to summer, along with skin
glistening with baby oil, another remedy, sunscreen or tanning lotion
to take effect as he practiced knocking home runs far into the woods
behind our house. More *good stuff.* Apple slices and shiny knuckles
on the rock porch—flat-faced boulders he'd set in mud to surround
the house, arranged carefully by shape to look like dinosaur tracks—
blending skin and skin and dirt, red.

Laughter, because the air is full of apple blossoms.
—Louise Glück, "Vita Nova"

IN THE AIR

For days, I declared that *the air is full of apple blossoms*, over and over and over in my twin bed, one wall from where my sister shouted some words of her own discovery in her half of the bunk bed we once shared. We'd earned the severing of that bunk bed set with age, having begun to blossom into our own skins; she'd swapped our mother's old bedroom for our brother's, closer to me. Poetry Out Loud had come to our small town, and the two of us, me small-voiced and her literature-averse, were set on finding perfect recitations to dazzle our English classes.

During this period, our bedroom doors remained comfortably open. Floating dust glittered by sunlight held a feeling of perceptible gentleness, when I knew very well how those same particles could menace on a day with less domestic cooperation, or more snow outside our green house, or a VHS tape repeatedly rewound and replayed rather than exchanged for another to mimic the forward motion of cable television. The electricity was on, some odd job for our father to clean some place overnight or build something had come through, and my sister and I found the energy to bear the brunt of dish and laundry maintenance. She found a poem about bears or something just as gruff, and her lines mingled with mine, repeated, over and over, until imprinted on my eyelids:

it is still spring, it is still meant tenderly.

I imagine, as we recited these poems and paced our wood-stained floors—the lines where our father had gotten tired, cleanly visible—loose white petals escaped the neighbor's crabapple tree to pass the road and enter our yard in trails of rural speed and meandering. We changed the tape when it was finished, and the memory became seasonally ambiguous.

Rosehip and Apple Jelly

Rosehips are a beautiful autumn fruit that punctuates country walks in November and December. There's no mistaking their small, oval, pillar-box shape and striking red fruit that hangs over hedgerows. They come from the same family as apples so it's no wonder that putting the two together results in a wonderful autumn hedgerow jelly. Any wild hips are perfect for this. They need to be ripe but don't have to be mushy, as several frosts will turn them.

BY THE WATER

They're like apples, Mia told me. Carmine-dotted hedges surrounded Squalicum Harbor between lavender-bush strokes. Our first spring.

We usually came to this place holding her black mop bucket. We'd dump wildflowers into its still-wet center, their rained-on petals mixing with remnants of soap. Purple sprigs would dust our knees and the sidewalk, lavender falling apart into confetti.

That day, we were only there for rosehips. Mia slid down grass to the water's ebbing edge and returned with several red-pink fruits. She opened one, scraped seeds and stinging hairs from the carcass, and passed it to me. I looked at the fresh-picked fruit like the dead body of a never-before-seen creature, uncertain of what life it could lead.

When we were in the area, we scoped out houses for their gardens, the last sprawled lavender before green gave way to yellow, yellow to orange, orange to brown. We managed to sneak away a couple miniature roses from one house—the part of the yard that could arguably qualify as sidewalk. By *we*, I mean I stayed in Mia's red Subaru, eyeballing a towering NO TRESPASSING sign while she took the same shears that we used to cut each other's hair to stems and thorns.

> *Knowing*
> *it wasn't ripe or sweet, I didn't eat*
> *but watched the other faces.*
> —Li-Young Lee, "Persimmons"

IN A DIFFERENT KITCHEN

When I was seventeen, my father remarried and moved to the other side of the country with me and my sister in tow. I did not find much to eat in our dim apartment during those first couple Washington years until I braved the fruit basket. We had one for the first time—a metal contraption from Walmart that held all the things I hadn't chosen before. Bananas, apples, kiwis, and navel oranges, unsteady in their mountain of peels at different thicknesses. They'd rot after weeks. I'd remember them once a month, finding each different skin mottled.

Once, as I unburdened myself of a bulging backpack, a ripe, green apple, the shape of a heart, the size of a fist, with the sturdiness of a worn baseball, caught my eye. I could treat it like plastic and pretend the skin was all there was, hollow core, artificial decoration to glance at and nothing more. Let it shine until there was no argument that it was deteriorating. Pretend, that inherited predisposition of mine.

Or I could bite. Find candy. Weight awkward in my hand. Chartreuse jolly rancher. I thought sour only came from junk food and preservatives, Sour Straws and Sour Patch Kids and sticky gummy granules that melted into each other like as-seen-on-TV slime, micro-beaded Floam, or at its realest, sweat through stubble. But this was a kind of candy that could go bad honestly, fold in on itself instead of going stale.

Rare Old Apples that Taste like Roses

If you plant a seed from an apple there's no guarantee you'll get fruit that's similar. Trees that grow from seeds often have fruit that's sour or bitter, sometimes almost inedible even. They're called "spitters" for good reason. In the past spitters and most all apples were primarily used for making apple jack liquor and hard ciders.

Sweet apples like we eat now are relatively new. They have become eating fruit mostly in the last century or two. To get the same tasting apple off a new tree, you graft a branch from the old tree onto new rootstock and grow a clone of the original apple.

IN ANOTHER WORLD

Mia and I didn't quite get around to the suit-and-tie fancy date with a bouquet of apples instead of roses. Before we found an apartment of our own, I bought more apples on grocery trips than I could ever eat. Gala for Mia, green for me. I'd throw one or two into my pocket when she picked me up. Every so often, a roommate would go through each tier of the hanging fruit basket to throw out what had gone bad, holding up the culprits to ask who was responsible. Every time, I got the blame for any apples. But if they were Jazz or Red Delicious, I knew there was more at play.

The first time we went to Canada, nineteen, we drank legal Rosé and tasted apple varieties from the Granville Island Market. Back at the AirBnB, we laid them out on tucked-in white bedding in an array of yellows and reds, shades which gradated but did not ever quite mix into the colors of sunset. Sweet: the apples glowing in the garden cottage, briefly ours. Tart: the unfamiliar cab trip back at night, when we lost the money from the ATM and accidentally stiffed the driver.

We had our Pink Lady next to Ambrosia, Envy, Pacific Rose. One-by-one, we laid bricks of gouda across our tongues, pauses between variations of sweetness.

It all came with us back over the border, apples awkwardly declared at crossing for a funny look from the patrol officer at their place on my lap in a plastic bag, their mention maybe out of necessity, but we hadn't crossed the border before, we didn't know. Holding them up for inspection felt like a declaration of something more.

> *Have you forgotten what we were like then*
> *when we were still first rate*
> *and the day came fat with an apple in its mouth*
> —Frank O'Hara, "Animals"

IN FAMILY

And the days came fast, with apple blossoms and apple kisses and apple skin, apple bouquets and apple declarations, apple jelly and apple imitations. Apples were in the fruit basket and in the passenger seat and in my father's hands and in my pocket and in my girlfriend's arms as she balanced our groceries at WinCo, and in the persimmons we got from WinCo because

of the Li-Young Lee poem I loved, and in the crabapples blown
into the creek by rough winds behind my childhood backyard,
swallowed by the surface, all skin. Apples red like sunburned
skin, and green like candy, and yellow like caution and time, and
flesh an opal of those things.

And the years came slow with stray apple blossoms
and the good stuff, and the line between artificial and organic
became less clear, and both could be sweet and sticky—part of
the same family.

Dive

It's super easy. I love it.

The whole family perched
above a black gulf.

Mom, her husband,   my sister,
our father's father. We are going

skydiving,
and I am so scared, but I am going
to do it. I don't like to do this kind of thing
alone.

I am so scared.
I am so scared.
I am so scared.

I pace—

but my grandfather, his barrel
body in slow-mo, rotates
towards me, towards the pit

after each soundless utterance:

It's super easy. I love it.

He does not let go in front of me, but I picture

his arms spread like

        oak leaves
            floating to the bottom
                of a deep crevice
                      where the earth has split

        open.

It's super easy.

We're in a large room like my old 4-H cabins,
bunk beds full of wealthy people,
        their fur coats.

It costs $80 to do a load of laundry here.

        It probably costs $80 to do a load of laundry
        there.

[Dryer broke
again. Half-done laundry drip-
ping tinted in winter, wood floor
molding. Dad's rough hands throwing
t-shirts, red rags caught on wall-hung
deer antlers, cigarette
voice going up in
smoke.]

The other families, with their money
in washing machines, they are solid.
Thick as mink and lamb, wet
                with the same water

      not in cold, sloppy pieces   like us.

My mother and her husband
      who always tells me   through his living-room cigarette
        that he is nothing like

                my father,

     and my grown-up little sister, who sees our father
     sometimes at Walmart but never waves.

These families don't go to Walmart, but I know
they have other ways to stay close.

I watch their laundry in the throes.

All that money spent
               the thrashing coats of wet animals
               against the washing machine window.

               It probably costs—

We roam
               the room, and we get in a black square car, and

my stepdad shows me
               his magnetic gun holder with the pistol

                              under the steering wheel.

                              I love it.

               He tries to pressure me into doing something else
               that scares me—

we have earmuffs, protection—

but my mom tells him I have been through a lot

[pinky fingers shoved in little ears for so long]

so he stops.

I know the gun demonstration is out of love.

I know it,
I know it,
I know it, but there's

another dad who isn't here

[red hands gloved in red ripped sleeves oiling
longer gun barrels on the living room couch]

TEENAGE BEDROOM:
"ELECTRICITY'S OUT"
EDITION

RATING ★ ★

Plain, comforting. This combination is eerily familiar, but it probably won't be your favorite.

> *Top Notes: Artificial vanilla, from-a-packet chicken broth, thin smoke*

> *Mid Notes: 50¢ Walmart candles, crinkled instant-ramen packaging, mildew*

> *Base Notes: Your father starting the basement wood burner, its metal door clanging coldly against everything unsaid, things you are used to but can't name*

TYPICAL BURN TIME DEPENDS ON YOUR HUNGER AND PATIENCE

REVIEW: You will come home from school to a dark house. This is not unusual. It's quite common for you to get off the bus and walk into the structure you call home cloaked in shadows: television off, father knocked out. The lack of energy radiates in all directions, the weight of wood walls and scratched floorboards sucking the life from every living thing inside. When you open the door, you feel it, too.

The creaking opening pulls your father's neck upwards as he delivers the news. *Power's out. They shut it off but I'm workin on it.*

He will probably say something like, *it won't be too long*, or *we'll be alright*. He'll descend to the basement with his coat.

Your sister will phone her friends and be gone soon enough, human escape routes on speed dial. Your brother will pace the garage indefinitely, crafting machines to power the family, drawing diagrams you don't understand. You won't ever remember how long the house stays dark. You will take what scraps of outside life you can: float your miserable self into a friend's parent's car, into each and every school dance because they are warm and the Little Caesars pizza is free. You won't call your father for a ride until the last guests have trickled out because there are whole boxes leftover at the end of the dance and your hands are as good as any to carry them out.

You'll get so tired of stale cupboard contents you'll try anything. Dig out the candles, find the smallest pot in the reeking kitchen mountain, pluck a ramen packet from the one reliable spot in the house. Balance it all, carefully. Leave a couple inches between each candle and place the pot's eroded enamel at the center, held up by each candle's glass lip. Make sure it doesn't snuff any of the wicks out. Brace the sink's frozen pipes for water. Watch.

Believe it will boil, even after twenty minutes have passed and you can cup the bottom of the pot in your hand and wonder if the dim warmth is emanating from it or from you.

Stare at the wall. Search the red quilt around your shoulders for tiny white protrusions that reveal themselves to be feathers pinched between your thumb and forefinger. Look back at the water. Wait. See a few bubbles forming in the scratches.

It will take almost as long as a Thanksgiving meal, anticipation and all. But in your hands, the pot will be warm—not hot. Just enough to slurp stringy noodles without burning your tongue.

*

What sense does it make?
On holidays that first year in college, I'll have the
whole dorm building to myself. No rigid returns
to mildew scent.

I'll learn later—in college, that people get flu shots
every year. That my teeth survived more than a decade
on their own. The dentist will scrape bricks of plaque
out of the space between my furthest tooth and tongue.

musk /*noun*

1. a substance with a penetrating persistent odor
obtained from a sac beneath the abdominal skin of
the male musk deer and used as a perfume fixative.

2. the odor of musk. also: an odor resembling musk
especially in heaviness or persistence.

Rewind: What scents of my own?

Musk: Cigarette smoke, cutoff cigarette filters, Dad's heavy army-green coats, the stuffy wall of air when I sleep at a friend's house and return to the smell a stranger.

Musk: The base note in the Sephora perfume samples Mom sends in the mail or keeps in the top dresser drawer for my visits. Labels say: *warm, inviting.*

Spill

for my sister

I'm sorry for saying you spilled chicken noodle soup on my spelling
book in sixth grade when the dog actually peed on it. Mrs. C handed
it back to me with a note where the ripped-off cover should be: *Yum!*
And for the times we served our piggy banks a feast, four courses
emptied from their stomachs for redigestion. My soccer-ball-painted,
dollar-store pig fought your basketball-pig for pennies and quarters, a
rudimentary redistribution of wealth except I was older and knew to go
for the quarters. I told you my pig was just hungry. You probably knew
that's why I could get so many plastic monkeys from the machines at
the front of Walmart.

I'm sorry I kept them all to myself, even after we carried two
carts full of groceries past the machines and loaded them in every
empty space in the back seat, bodies indistinguishable from the bags
around our knees. The more they rustled, the more Daddy ran sweat
upward through his hair in the front seat, and that's all any of us could
see beyond the outline of his stubble. Strands on ceiling like static
except stickier. Donut box crushed by his knuckles on the dashboard
with bakery fluff still inside but packed so tight, like how we'd roll white
bread into balls in our palms when we were younger except not at all
the same. I kept the monkey or puppy or plastic prize in my palm but
forgot about it the second we left those sliding doors, receipt trailing
from the perspiring grip of his fist, SNAP balance at the bottom making
an *O,* his huff and puff like the last breath of something run dry. I'm
sorry I got so angry at you for asking for Twizzlers or McDonald's or the
gaming keyboard in Best Buy that one time he got a paycheck and I got
so scared it would disappear but more scared that *he* would—behind

grease and calluses, mullet like a mane, the rest of him roaring, volume of grief or frustration (or whatever feeling smashes donuts inside a paper box without ripping the paper) as explosive as his laughter, two moods hard enough to tell apart that we could go back to normal the minute we carried everything inside, knowing that it would happen again, again, when the next thing ran out and he couldn't fill the space but he could sure fill the silence.

It was easy to pin the soiled spelling book on you, knit excuses from excess of warmth, a home meal, instead of the lack. I stuffed my pinkies so deep in my ears it was easy to forget you heard him, too. When we came home to the knowledge that we would not be going anywhere yet, not today, that there was no new money and a new possible date of eviction, it was simpler to fill each other's ears, relieve the tension with a walk out the back door, tell you how *Mrs. C had so much more energy than usual because the superintendent sat in on fifth period* all while we were still moving, hardly taking the time to throw our backpacks off before we were through the yard and the woods and down the trail to the stream where it was quiet except for the water in and around our shoes, Converse-canvas submerged, a lone crabapple dropping into water so clear we could see the river taste it.

Some solutions only work in daylight.

I'm sorry I expected him to let the dog out in the pitch black, when we were double-blanketed and he was propped up watching *Groundhog Day*. I'm sorry it took so long to hear her whimper.

Heluva

after Craig Santos Perez' "SPAM's carbon footprint"

Heluva Good! Extra Sharp Cheddar Cheese exists at the exact midpoint between yellow and orange, wrapped in green, the shade of every block and folder and sheet of construction paper from elementary school that no one, even people who love green, would ever call their favorite. **Heluva Good!** was founded by Perry Messinger of Sodus, New York in 1925. **Heluva Good!** is fast-food substitute and pitstop at Pap's house—Uniontown, Pennsylvania, big house on the hill (although when I say hill, I'm not sure if I mean up or down, just that the yard swerves all over, trimmed, with a large barrel just a dot in the expanse of grass, brown metal smoking with cardboard, plastic wrap, **Heluva!** lot of trash). **Heluva Good!** began as washed cheese curd hobby in the basement of A.B. Williams Company, or so Wikipedia says, and Wikipedia does not mention A.B. Williams Company anywhere except in the **Heluva Good!** article, and Google searches give me the possibilities of A.B. Williams existing either as construction or cereal company. We ate **Heluva Good!** in that house with the orange shag carpet (except for the one room, once my youngest uncle's bedroom, where cheddar steps were traded for green, something between mint and **Heluva!** wrapper). **Heluva Good!** tastes divine paired with a six-pack of single-serve Pepsi bottles divvied up into four short glasses and blue-dappled mugs, a feeling always accessible as long as there is a **Good!**will or flea market around to pick up a couple handheld portals to Pap's house. Executive officers listed for the **Heluva Good!** company: *President: Father Time, Treasurer: Death and Taxes, Secretary: Geo. Experience.* We ate **Heluva Good!** without crackers, although saltines were certainly offered, the single food that didn't run out. Brother would slice—alternating between almost-translucent slivers and opaque oblongs, whether we could see through to the other side simple luck of the draw. Hands lifted small pieces to set them back down with crooked teeth imprints, little bubbles of spit, bite not quite clean. We ate **Heluva Good! Extra Sharp Cheddar Cheese** without knowing we were downing the kind of sharpness you absorb more than see. We ate **Heluva Good!** and looked out the kitchen balcony to grazing deer below without ever exiting the door in unspoken understanding that our bodies would crash through the aging floorboards. We ate **Heluva Good!** and heard all about Pap's girlfriends from the senior center who drove him to the gas station or the grocery store and about the money Uncle Rich lost gambling. We ate **Heluva Good!** after *visitation* with our mother, on the days there was no money for Wendy's but time to postpone the two-hour drive home for contributions to the coffee-table thousand-piece puzzle of some blue sky or some burnt canyon, time for a walk through the garage to see all the latest things Pap's been cleaning out (except every visit, there's an old bike we haven't seen, a new stained couch, an unfamiliar water-ringed coffee table). *I got a **Heluva** deal on these chairs, and I'm gonna sell em to that guy cross the road.* **Heluva Good!** made its mark in chilled aisles with the packaged cartoon face of Father Time. I escaped that kitchen table for the bathroom where everything was blue: blue sink, blue tub, blue walls, blue toilet with blue water. I walked downstairs and out the front door and picked rocks from the driveway but not the blue one in the walkway. I treaded backyard barrel smoke and glanced at the neighbor's blue swimming pool and swam up one hill to the rope swing and tiptoed on sand just before the ground dropped, too scared to let myself go. **Heluva Good!** made its mark in small slices in my small hands with the face of Father Time. I walked into the garage and found it empty. I went to the stairs behind the bikes and descended into the basement. There was my father, just standing there, where the empty eggplant carpet still sunk under long-gone furniture. There was my father's father and his charcoal voice: *I walked in the woods out back the other day and found a man living down there.* He might've said he left him be. He didn't have to say he was going to go play his number at the gas station after we left. His Powerball signature blurs in my memory with Dad's, familiar angel number 5 5 5.

I Picture Something Alive

a man covered in something blue, something
        spiking out from his body in the way things do when pulled
        away—thinning into a point

I am small, waking up on the floor of an empty room
        dim-dark   cool-cold

the man sneering, his body
        a sticky blue-black, as if a bruise found its way out
            of the skin but not its way apart

        I am downstairs
            a screen curves out from a little TV
        Ashton Kutcher in *Dude, Where's My Car*

      the kitchen mixes my divorced grandparents
      my mother's side—
            chairs encased in maternal plastic, table piled
high in receipts, grandfather's toy slot machine
      stickered cherry and triple banana
            Ziplocked garden peppers thawing out in yellows

the blue man's not on the TV
I'm not downstairs—I'm in the attic
      I've never seen the attic, the tiny door behind the floor-length door
            that held my father's guns, the ones
        in the closet that didn't lock, even though

　　　　　there were other cabinets full of guns that did
lock

I am small—I picture the room full
　　　　　　　　of bats and rolling dust, a wood-plank floor
　　　　with holes in it, though there are no holes
　　　　　　　　in our ceiling

I picture something alive

　　　　　　　　　that I can't quite picture, my father's heavy
　　　　metal songs: *Rock Mr. Spock, The Wizard Tree,*
how he said he toured in Sweden and I've wanted

to believe him, his mullet greased black
　　　　　　　　　in the cold, his red hands
　　　　running strands in spikes up to the roof

our overindulgence of the food stamps
the way home from Walmart

I tell the food stamp lady I don't know
the make of my truck, still haven't learned to
drive it, just got it to convince my girlfriend's parents
I have a sense of freedom

Mom used to cut up Slim Jims with scissors
and give me a bowl like little dog treats

I watch the Slim Jim man
his meaty hair
thinning

Overscrambled

for Mia

I pull my bread, sourdough, from the yellow metal breadbox—yours, also sourdough, from the freezer. I place your slice in the toaster to the left with four different settings, on *frozen*, mine in the toaster to its right with a single-handle push. I lay out two pans for two different kinds of sausage, and beside one kind (for which the label does not list *wheat*), I also add an egg over vegetable oil.

Over medium: The egg is flipped, and the yolk is only slightly runny.

You make fun of how I crack it—gentle taps around the egg's circumference with the inner membrane slowly making its way across my fingertips, as if to peel and not break open. You like your eggs over medium. For a long time, I didn't know what that meant—Mom cooked scrambled or *flat* eggs, the former mixed on the pan with milk and butter, the latter mixed in a bowl and simply left on the pan for a few minutes to form a yellow crêpe. She does the same now with pancake mix when I visit her kitchen with the copper sink in Finleyville, batter pulled from the skillet in thin layers like skin.

She visits us in Bellingham and sits at our kitchen table confessing tales of the past—Dad and the divorce, the lawsuit after he lost his job/was wrongfully fired/*I won't ever truly know if he was wrongfully fired because I was so little back then and my instinct was to defend him because that's what you do for your dad*, the lawsuit he won anyway. The settlement money that bought the new white car and box-set DVDs, Walmart carts stacked with non-food splurges, money's brief appearance eclipsed by impulse and sandwiched by years of hunger.

This is the first time you hear the echo in my mother's voice: *He just always knew how to get what he wanted.*

Visitation meetups at the giant Paul Bunyan statue outside the tire place, giant Las Vegas tote bags gifted to me and my siblings the Christmas after she married our stepdad. Bags that held all the favorite clothes we brought for the weekend and eventually crunched to nothing in the dryer, printed text flaking off into wordless eggshell.

Scrambled: The egg is beaten, heated, then stirred gently.

I am quiet as she reveals, remembering how, when she picked us up at one of the midway points and my brother or sister started dissing on our father, I insisted that everyone *shut up*. I wanted to say he was doing his best, but I wasn't on either side—when he started up with *god-your-mother-is-just-so,* I advocated for neutrality. For once, I just wanted everyone to be quiet.

Maybe I should have seen it coming, that we would end up this way. You only ever meeting half of the family, you wondering what my dad looks like outside of that single blurry image on my phone where he's posing with cardboard Edward in the *Twilight*-themed visitor's center in Forks, and me wondering after the years, too.

I make everyone scrambled eggs with New Woman cheese and sprinkled Fontina, updates to Mom's recipe, no milk. By my hand, the eggs solidify, freckling where the cheese hits its crisping point. I still prepare them in tub-scoops of butter just like Mom does.

She's just relieved I can cook a little. Her worry is easy.

Over easy: The egg is flipped, and the yolk is still runny.

When your mom visits, I swirl the eggs in vegetable oil and rely on garlic powder for the taste. You remind me that she doesn't eat cheese while I am in the middle of cooking; I didn't get it out in the first place. Your family eats every egg with molten insides, but your mom says these are the best she's ever had.

You like your eggs over medium, not over easy. Each time I perform this ritual, I must restrain myself from solidifying these spilling gold rays into hot sun, and half of the time, I do anyway—too often stepping away to fill our Brita filter or wash raspberries in the new dollar-store mesh strainer or to set some dirty dish to the side of the sink like putting it there is just as good as cleaning it, too often returning to a callused sphere of yellow.

Sunny side up: The egg is fried with the yolk up and is not flipped.

Dad used to talk about sunny-side-up eggs but didn't make them. I could only imagine how they might warm on a skillet when we visited the kitchen of his father's house, my eyes zeroing in on that old diner booth that mounted the home phone among newspapers and old photos that scrambled more than they told. I wonder if that's where they ate breakfast as a family. Did he grow up there? Or was that home a stranger to his childhood self?

My father's hands were better at carrying the eggs inside from the gas station and handing them off to me, still in their cardboard carton, than they were at cracking them.

When I get your breakfast right, using the metal spatula with the pale-blue handle and the windowpane openings you like, I scoop it as if to turn the egg on its side in sleep, let white wrap over yolk like bedcovers on every millimeter of skin. I lift it up and out of the pan— each second a risk—and onto your plate, setting it beside the first one I accidentally hardened, this one hot water, trying my best not to pop it, to layer it on your gluten-free toast with strawberry jam and gouda and sausage and turkey bacon even though the sour smell sometimes makes me sick—and eggs, too, actually, since I ate so many of them for a year or two of my life back in that green house you haven't been to, twice daily sizzling scrambled-egg sandwiches on wheat bread and orange American wax slices beside the piled silver sink, when I made the eggs with oil, trying to figure out how my mother served them when she still lived in the same house, before the divorce, before the questions of *how on earth did that man get custody.* All those sandwiches sweated onto my lap as I watched the full DVD cases of *Seinfeld* Dad got from FYE on a bulky TV in that stuffy bedroom, my skin peeling with sunburn or December.

Sometimes, we eat in front of our big TV, the one that your coworker at your old job gave you for free, watching *The Good Doctor* and *9-1-1* with our breakfast in our laps on a Sunday morning. Oil for your eggs, butter for mine. No sweat.

Over well: The egg is flipped, and the yolk is cooked hard.

I lift that egg on your plate for you to say, *Wow, you actually made me breakfast today?* I lift that egg beside your toast and bacon last because it's the first thing to go cold off the stove. I lift that egg with soft-serve hands and try not to pop it, not after I just hardened the first, although I will do both more times than I can count, the skillet already yellow rock, your plate spilling with yolk guts.

RED HOT CHILI PEPPERS
SWEATSHIRT

RATING ★ ★ ★ ★ ★

Feel the brand-new fleece lining in front of your blurry bedroom mirror. Newness against your skin like the goosebumps it breaks out in when your cold arms hit burning bathwater.

> *Top Notes: Hot Topic, Body Fantasies vanilla spray, Great Value laundry detergent*
>
> *Mid Notes: Stained sleeve cuffs, Chips Ahoy cookie crumbs*
>
> *Base Notes: Sephora perfume samples mailed by your mom with manly odors of wood and musk, what you imagine it feels like to hibernate*

TYPICAL BURN TIME IS AS LONG AS IT TAKES FOR YOU TO GROW OUT OF IT

REVIEW: You don't remember when you bought the sweatshirt, but you do remember pulling it on by the space heater, static in winter. Cumberland's Country Club Mall is at least an hour drive—where your classmates go for their ever-growing collections of Bath and Body Works that suffocate you in the school halls. You have to drive two hours if you want to go anywhere that appeals to your taste—the soon-to-be-abandoned Century III Mall in West Mifflin where you bought the last copy of *One Flew Over the Cuckoo's Nest* when maybe only three stores were open but the indoor carousel still carried your siblings' pale limbs in unhurried fluorescent-lit circles while you followed on your own still animal.

No matter what occasion spurs the shopping trip—a sleepover at a friend's house, leaving the weekend from your mother's, or somehow having coaxed a family trip from home—your bedroom is going to be cold when you get back.

The first thing you do is turn on the space heater. Watch dust between each metal rung float off as you push it towards the outlet under the wall mirror. In front of that mirror, you pick at your skin, check to make sure both of your earrings are still in—ensuring that the mechanical pencil erasers you stuffed the wires into are holding them tight. This time, you prioritize softness over warmth. You pull out the brand-new red sweatshirt with the logo in the center, a shape like a star trying to be a first aid symbol. Against skin that's been sandpapered by pilled sweaters in a lineage of hand-me-downs, it reinvents you.

Postpone washing as long as possible. Pull the collar up to your nose after wearing it for days to check that you are not moving in a cloud of body odor. Sure enough, the new smell has waned, but in its place, you find remnants of Walmart vanilla or Mom's Sephora samples. Mixed with sweat from the times you choose comfort over logic in gym class and keep the sweatshirt on to run the mile, its red like a flag to get you pummeled by your peers who establish their weight in how many laps they can rack up for the PACER test.

Wash it finally. Notice grease stains, others. Forget to fold it, wear another sweater. Lose the red one. Come back to the smell months later, years—the one thing your sister, before she, too, is out of there, manages to save of your things. Wonder how she snuck it out—some day after you left for college, when your father and his wife carried what life you'd left in boxes out to the parking lot dumpster. That smell, now a stranger.

*

Final Notes: Classify Something Recognizable

Honeysuckle: What have I sugarcoated?

Baked Cookies: What have I made on my own? Of my own?

Sweet Bourbon: Where do I escape to?

Maple Syrup: What are my extravagances?

Musk: How do I define my upbringing?

Salt (and other verbs)

transitive verb; to treat, provide, or season with common salt
salt the food
salt a driveway

Crush

I hate saltines. Square pillows in square boxes on a square shelf in
the kitchen that should have been a bookshelf but lines the wall with
soup cans and untouched saltines. The kitchen where my mother
twists wire into bracelets and wind-spinners and pieces to find years
later. Beginnings to unearth after farmers' market fame, beginnings
to unearth after she has long left the green house for another,
beginnings in wire spirals and loops and chain-link stomped by steel-
toe boots or kept in jewelry boxes that get emptied into totes and
knocked over by cats and things that just disappear the way they do
when suddenly I am twenty-one and I haven't seen those crammed
walls or my father in years.

Vomit

Everything is streetlights. The kind after a wedding, after midnight,
that make my mother puke on the drive home. She says she just can't
handle all the bright flashes when it's dark—they blur the road ahead,
gush fluorescence, and spike out in glimmers that confuse the edges
of the world still alive with the night's heaving black. I will understand
this, slowly, in the next ten years, as my own vision deteriorates. But
here, I am younger than ten. This is the only wedding I have ever
been to (Dad's brother is the groom, but Dad stayed home to rewind-
replay-rewind *Field of Dreams*).

Love

I love weddings. Probably. Or Valentine's Day. Heart shapes. Hold onto a heart-shaped flip mirror bedazzled red and treasure that oversimplification of romantic affairs. Dance with the bride at my uncle's wedding. (She is the bride more than she is my aunt). My grandfather ties dollar bills into bows and passes them out to all the kids in line to trade for a dance, and then to trade twirls and waltzes for a slice of vanilla cake in a plastic takeaway box.

I keep a heart-shaped chocolate box, one of the ones my mother and stepdad send home with me to West Virginia, propped on top of bedroom desk scribbles in a year-round shrine to St. Valentine. I am thirteen, fourteen, fifteen and celebrating with 99¢ bottles of sparkling water purchased from Walmart, pitstops with my father on the dark drive home from *visitation*. I sip for days on hints of strawberry and lime.

Look

Look in the mirror and see my mother.
Look in the streetlights as if to see my father.

Run

Remember saltines as mouthfuls of plaster. The food card running out. Pooling pennies for white bread and hiding it in my bedroom. Raiding my supply (and my sister's) and trying my brother's room to find the door locked. Braving the kitchen bookshelf for stale squares.

Find

I won't direct anyone to our pockets. Pockets—burrows. Stuff that doesn't expire. Tree-trunk holes or air bubbles of backup snacks, potato chip bags in gun cabinets. Closets that used to hold my mother's jewelry boxes (jewelry boxes that once held untouched earring studs and Ziploc-baggied baby teeth), closets that used to have doors now hung with stapled transparent curtains to veil plastic tubs of picture frames and rubber toys from Walmart machines, rusted jewelry, and sometimes a box of Rice Krispies Treats. Gun cabinets sometimes held by lock and key but most of the time simply avoided. Inside, boxes of purple and white Good & Plentys shiver like ruptured blood vessels around the real treasure: off-brand peanut butter sheltered from my brother's nut allergy.

Write

These are the things I won't write about.

Dig

Pockets on the garage floor where two-liters of Twist Up and RC breathe through laundry basket holes, washed up on kitchen steps in waves of t-shirts and bedsheets. Pockets in outdoor sheds where night air holds Coca-Cola cans cold. Pockets under my bed with blue-and-yellow Kraft cups, red-and-yellow Slim Jim boxes with loose sticks escaping to the floor, and less-edible things such as baking soda and nutmeg to remedy my acne. Pockets in my sister's room that change places every time I look. Pockets locked away under my brother's bed with room-temp lemonade.

Salt

I haven't thought so much about saltines, but I have thought about salt. In college, someone discourages me from including McDonald's in a poem. I do not try to justify it. *It's just a detail*, I say.

In high school, when the internet gets shut off, Dad takes me to McDonald's to write love letters on their wi-fi. He doesn't know of my teenage long-distance romance—we are here for a McDouble, or we are here for nothing at all—it's just beside the gas station on the way home from Walmart. I lose my first love when the connection goes bad.

Someone tells me, if you ask the workers for fries without salt, *they have to make a whole new batch*. Guaranteed fresh fries. But I am fine with them cold. The best ones are lying stiff at the bottom of the bag. Dad moves us across the country for a way out. The scenery changes; the evergreens get taller; the slick cardboard containers of McDonald's fries congeal the air of a different fridge with the sense of rest only found in grease.

I break through the grease. I write love letters on paper to a different girl years after her first job at McDonald's. She tells me they wanted her to stay, forget college. But she is here, and I am going to that college she refused to forget. We sit on the couch and red-and-yellow commercials tell us, *We butter every bun*. She scoffs. *No, they don't*.

Derive

I am nineteen, then twenty. Before we sit on the couch, we sit on her bed. Mia's wall-collage tells me everything. One simple black-and-white piece of paper taped to the wall on the side of her bed reads, HOW TO DERIVE THE MAXIMUM ENJOYMENT FROM CRACKERS. There are no steps. I decide to introduce her to my mother. It will take nearly a year with college and the distance, but that year is peppered with Snapchat conversations between the two of them.

Leave

I tell myself I still have my mother because she left in the divorce. Because her leaving was a renewal, a getting-away from my father, even when his way with words kept us kids on his side. Maybe those years would have been better if she had been the one feeding us every day. But I know for how long she was too anxious to challenge him, how she kept paying child support for all three kids years after the older two of us had already turned eighteen and started our own lives.

I tell myself I still have my mother because she left our father, but she never left us. Even her every-other-weekend McDonald's stops were different—only at my request on the two-hour drive to her house or returning to our green house from the farmers' market, ten-piece chicken nuggets and large fries and barbecue sauce lids that I stuck on car doors without meaning to, somehow magnetized. I have only seen her order from McDonald's once or twice for herself, an egg or some lettuce-y thing on a side menu that's supposed to sound healthy. But she would take me at my worst, teenaged and bratty, thinking I'd die without those nuggets.

She only half-knew what we ate, how we ate, at home. She'd ask questions, but if my father's words were bold, italicized—hers were only dotted lines, a tiptoe kind of prying.

I tell myself I still have my mother because she didn't mind all that much. Because she'd buy me a hash brown in the morning to keep me from complaining and take all her metal and plop it down twice a week next to tables piled with rhubarb and blackberries, then hand me a fresh-from-the-bank five-dollar bill out of her change bag to get something homemade. Because she was a highlight of the Mountain Fresh Farmers Market even if you spent only five minutes strolling the booths. Her presence added the sound of silverware not scraping or cutting or feeding, but clanging and clinging onto one another, gently— spoons and forks dangling with chain-link and beads in recycled windchimes on a carved wooden tree display my father had built and wood-stained for her years and years before, when it was all just a hobby.

When I go back, I sit behind her farmers' market booth like I am seven, ten, thirteen again, and I am too shy to walk across the pavilion and meet the eyes of Judy in our two-dollar-and-fifty-cent exchange for a caramel icing cinnamon roll. Judy is still there. The rug lady is not, but the vendor that took her place sells wool like she did. Wood people, honey people, specific farmers who all manage to sell everything anyone could ask for—they're all still there. And my mother still selects cucumbers with pen-marked fingers in the day's last minutes.

Ground

There are too many characters. Need to ground them. The facts:

My mother says she can't cook, but I used to love her breadsticks before I left out a cup of Little Caesars marinara in the bedroom and started to gag every time I saw red sauce.

My father used to bring home two full baskets of McDonald's fries as a treat. The day he discovered you could ask for shiny red baskets in the drive-through was a revelation.

Mia likes to meal prep but says I do not seem like a *leftovers person*. She is not wrong, but I get defensive. *Of course* I'm a leftovers person. I just don't remember to heat anything up until there's already fuzz thickening on the Tupperware lid.

I practice the important words with remnants of food—the word *lesbian* squeezed over my tongue in Minute Maid orange juice before I ever tell anyone, *I love you* washing down stale crackers with water. If I say it empty-mouthed, my throat sputters.

Write

I write: my love, my father, my mother, my grandfather with the wedding dollar bills tied into bows and at his home, his brown paper bag of losing lottery tickets. All those years spent under the guidance of *Did you know? You can turn in all these peeling, grease-stained things when you win, and they will cut that out of what you have to pay in taxes*. When you win. When Dad had money, he took us to a Uniontown Wendy's after picking us up from weekend visits at Mom's; when he did not, he took us to his dad's house. We drank Pepsi, sliced green-wrapped orange Heluva cheddar. Our grandfather gently offered saltines when his tube of plain Pringles ran out, and I said no most days in a way I couldn't to myself in our own empty kitchen.

Salt

My mother loves pink Himalayan salt. She used to say she didn't get it—why anyone would pay the extra. Something changed when she met my stepdad, when she moved to that house in Pennsylvania and got her own workshop in the basement. No more wire at the dinner table. No, we eat at this dinner table. And we eat *pink salt*. On salad, mingling with red wine vinegar on the wet hearts of iceberg lettuce with no brown spots, just a bit of garlic powder and dark specks of pepper.

So much relief to see pepper and know it's pepper. Living in fear of black dots in my food for so long, the non-stick coating of Dad's favorite Goodwill skillets flecking into my scrambled eggs, the black spatula disintegrating under heat. Or maybe the dots something still edible but just *old*, crusted food not scrubbed enough with Dawn or Joy, bittering today's food with something we'd burned long before.

Crush

Google *crushed saltines* because I do not know any other way to ground my writing. Find recipes before image evidence. Baked Saltine Cracker Chicken. Cracker Crumb Chicken Tenders. Crunchy Saltine Chicken Tenders.

Place crackers into freezer Ziploc baggie. Crush with rolling pin until they're a coarse crumb. Are saltines a key ingredient in *any* recipe that values them whole?

Salt/Ground

I include McDonald's in a poem anyway, but this time, it's about my mom. Or it's about germs, the world filling with Clorox and hand-sanitizing wipes, the grocery stores emptied, for the first time, of canned soups. I can't help but wonder now if anyone picked up the crackers, if they preserve the same way.

But the germs—rewinding further back, further, further, Mom's refusal to let me even enter the indoor playgrounds at McDonald's. I am six. She admonishes against those snot- and disease-ridden primary-colored tubes. Twisting squishy fries in my fingers on the other side of the glass, pricking paper cuts with little salt granules.

Ground

My mother hasn't ever been a big proponent of fast-food sodium, but she always told me to eat saltines when I felt my stomach turning. I hold them in my hand. It is enough to feel the edges. One, two, three, four. Corners. One, two, three, four. Divide one up into four bites. One, two, three, four.

Love

The first thing I cook for myself—*really* cook—no box mixes or frost-covered cardboard directions or bags or anything with inner packets of something like dust, comes from the farmers' market. I have to go home for it. Cross the country for Pennsylvania and West Virginia and the middle path through that little bite of Maryland, states that divided my time between custody agreements. The Mountain Fresh pavilion does not provide much comfort for my mother and I on a foggy, wet Wednesday after my first year of college except in smell—petrichor turning to broth and wafting us to sample cups at the 4-H table, tiny puddles textured by lentils, carrots, mushrooms, spinach. The next day, I walk into my mother's house from a summer job reeking of gas station pizza, and she has all the broth to cover the smell. We drink the Tupperware dry in days.

That fall, I make it for my roommates. Spend hours listening to French music and discovering that people really do cry from onions. Realize that I haven't ever gotten that close to one before. The next spring, I make it with my girlfriend, and she chops all the carrots larger than I would like them, but I only double-chop a few when she's finished. We offer the soup to Mia's roommates, but they won't eat any. They order McDonald's again. They are so impressed that we *cook*. Sometimes, they still offer fries to Mia and me, but she is finally making up for all those years ignoring her body, vomiting nightly, and she is quitting gluten for good this time, and Mia knows one hundred percent that McDonald's uses the same fryers for everything, and if she takes them up on it, she will throw those well-intentioned offers up later. So we drink our soup leftovers until the round container blocks out the rest of our dinner desires and finally decide a little waste is okay.

Summer, I make the soup while Mia is at work and for some reason wash/chop the mushrooms up first, and they turn the whole kitchen into the thready underbelly of a forest log, and I have no idea if that's just how they smell and usually I do the onions first so they cover up any mossy beginnings or if maybe I should throw them all out. The soup is perfect, but we still don't eat it all.

Fall, I forget about the recipe.

Winter, we make it again and spoon-slurp until I pull a rock out of my teeth. Comb through every following bite with my tongue, scared to crack anything open, scared to swallow, wondering which vegetable carried the rock into my apartment, if maybe the leeks held a tiny nest of rocks within their rings. We freeze the soup. I work up the courage to heat up a bowl only once, but Mia takes it for her lunch every day this week.

Love

One, two.

Love

Hiding angelfish saltshakers in the picnic basket until Mia's birthday. WinCo pepperoni and Mt. Olive pickles and talks about getting married under willows, different types of gouda and sometimes McDonald's fries, raspberry hats on our fingertips, the air smelling of saltwater.

Love

Moving with Dad to the West Coast, taking my first gulps of saltwater. First weeks in a motel room, first nights in the apartment on laundry molded into makeshift mattress. Dad disappearing to work, his first routine since I've been able to remember. Dad and stepmom disappearing after work for hours, too. Grocery trips no longer shared. Dad teaching me to drive in the white car, only a few times between my usual city-bus rides, on a winding road beyond the town, towering evergreens swallowing everything I'd known before. Pulling up to McDonald's before home to the stuffy apartment. My father's hands and shoulders stranger than they used to be. New light across the dashboard, across his paler hands, glinting through the salt that leaves the fries for his skin.

I share my college application essay with him—an early, tell-all version, titled *Home*—and he loves it, but he tells me that the things I'm writing about are not things everyone needs to know. He moves on. Talks about the news, what he heard from Alex Jones.

Write

I write: the thin, salted edge between truth and what I'm allowed to tell, family figures hulking in my nightmares. I end college with a class called *Poetry & Dreams*: dream journal entries as writing material. I tell my childhood through poems with the images twisted around my fear, the Slim Jim grease turned blue and black. The Walmart aisles and plates—empty.

Love

Bringing my mother to pick smooth rocks from saltwater, her first time on a plane so much later than mine. She leaves them with me to mail back to her when she goes home, souvenirs she will later wrap in wire.

Write

A handwritten receipt for farmers' market goat cheese, twelve dollars for a tangy third of my palm. I don't remember the name of the specific kind I like except that it's pale yellow with an orange rind. I am seven, ten, nineteen, twenty-one. I beg my mother for it, beg the farmers' market bell that rings every morning at 10 AM for it, tuck single dollar bills into my pockets and save for it, beg for years until I've outgrown my pockets, and this time, I'm begging Mia to try a sliver of goat cheese from the sample bin at Fred Meyer even though she hates the aftertaste.

Bite into that little cheese triangle and leave crooked marks where my front teeth bolt in different directions. Bite apples this way. Peel open Oreos and leave the same indentations in their icing. I try it with other foods, but saltines only shatter.

MY OWN PRIVATE
WEST VIRGINIA

RATING NOT APPLICABLE

Sweet honey drizzles memory like cough syrup, enough to create a multi-sense experience. Best for new residents of Washington state, this scent walks you through your homesickness.

> *Top Notes: Raw honey, spiced apple, burning wood*
>
> *Mid Notes: Maple syrup, a hint of mold, a hint of cigarette smoke*
>
> *Base Notes: Frozen groceries and fast-food wrappers, pizza boxes in the wood burner, every closed door, an open copy of* Generation Dead, *a well-loved article of clothing, a place to miss*

TYPICAL BURN TIME IS STILL UNDER REVIEW

REVIEW: Your mother mails you goat's milk soap from the farmers' market where she sells jewelry, her booth a half hour away from your West Virginia hometown and crossing state lines into Maryland. Spiced Apple and Peach is a past favorite that lengthened your showers, but this year, she just sent Peach. It somehow smells just like the grass on that side of the country.

Your father texts you and is no more involved than he's ever been, but he leaves a voicemail one day. Sound you haven't heard in years ignites olfactory muscle memory, and in his cadence, there's the cheap, greasy McDoubles and decades of cigarette smoke that feel like love, and you don't know how to put into words why. In breathy, recorded fuzz, you recognize the wood walls that made your old home a perpetual mountaintop getaway.

It doesn't matter so much anymore. But it's second nature—conflating bathwaters, vanilla-scented things, maple, all the notes. Working a summer job at a pharmacy that plays *Take Me Home, Country Roads* in its regular rotation, some love for that song carried into Washington, the only other to share the rhododendron state flower. Mistaking customers who pay in pennies for your dad. Controlling your impulses when it comes to packaged facial masks, bath bombs, articles of comfort. Shelving candles for the fall display, you forget about the hole in the shopping cart when you fill it with new items to put out, shattering three maple candles in quick succession as they fall through, before you know what's coming.

Carry the lumps of brown wax into damages. Contemplate just taking them home.

I Stopped Dreaming

Her hands on her Mustang wheel

new things wrapped in velvet,
folded limbs, off-kilter Little Dipper. I coughed

so much syrup, bullfrogs blackening
under the tucks of tires: sounds were different then

another name for a name outgrown; in poems
what's become: *father* and in stories: *Dad*
but together we just say *he*

a whisper almost capital. Last we lived here
we buried turkeys in feet of snow
little grocery netting around the ankles
cutting flake
by flake. *She's living*

in a cool green farmhouse or
she's tattooed the wrong longitude
wrong mountain range
a single footprint

misplaced—it was coldest

the winter we weren't there.

We weren't daughters, just girls.

Slept in glaciers. Salamander bones beneath the maple.

Almost pretty. But I lie to you, lie
shivering.

Notes on Preservation

Cauterize the stems and the sap stays inside, keeps them pretty, keeps decay away for another day or two or three. At least that's what you heard about poppies. Now you think you can do it to everything, like the calla lilies that begin to kneel only a few days after you buy the plant, golden heads bowing to follow legs going soft.

You can't just let them die. You pull black roots out of the pot (or Mia does because you can't stand to feel how they've turned to mush in your care) and try to untangle, but it all looks the same, and you don't know your way around wires, so how can you know which cut is the cure-all?

Repot, add rocks for drainage, but still no fix.

The issue can't be overwatering because you only just bought them, remember, but it isn't neglect because their stems are elastic, pulpy, like maybe they have enough to drink but it's the wrong thing, or the wrong pot, the wrong acrylic eggplant paint on terracotta and maybe you blocked their airways by Mod Podge-sealing it—

and anyway, if you cauterize the stems the sap stays inside, keeps them pretty, keeps in the water you might have suffocated them with. You get to them just in time to preserve their heads. Take lime-green Bic lighter to the point where each neck connects and watch sap burn, sizzle. Do it to all five—you only lost one when it doubled over and fell to the floor at your first caress of its unique mono-petal, leaving you shocked at your own touch.

Cover the bottom of a Tupperware in silica sand. Flood every crevice and coat the spadix, porous granules to turn blooms paper-thin.

Mia says you should do it to poppies, like you'd heard about. She mentions this on the drive past the roundabout full of them because they disintegrate after a day in a vase on the table. But you can't look at them the same way, not after that dream where you microwaved bright sunrise Californias and picked them from the plate, one by one, until remembering with matter-of-fact dream knowledge that this was a recipe for death, and suddenly there you were, holding limp stems like reheated french fries, a dozen already in your stomach.

You'd rather do it to another lily, another calla, this time snipped from a yard down the street, and you know you probably shouldn't have done it, and this one is white and luminous and that bell-shaped petal is so large that the brown spot on the corner is hardly noticeable (you surely didn't see it from the street), but maybe if you lived in that house you would dwell on it, pick the bloom apart by the hour.

You don't really know what you'll do with it—it's a bit big for Tupperware, and you haven't tried to hang dry any of these lilies just yet—but guilt arises when you take flame to stem and it's far too thick to burn easily, so you cut it just a bit higher to get to the thin spot, but taking scissors to this stem is like biting through your pinky, which you can't do, you guess, because your body won't let you,

and you can't cut this lily, because your body won't let you,

and the poppies are in your stomach,

and you have tried too hard to keep the sap inside.

You can cauterize the stem and listen to it sizzle for a full five or fifteen minutes, or you can let the end dry like bad pieces of asparagus you throw out at dinner, or you can give up on the backbone, cut off the head, bury what you can in silica until it's sucked dry and paper-thin, until the sand's blue speckles turn pink with taken water, until what's left of the bloom is so light that this chrysalis return gives

all the air in the world

to carry it.

My Brother's House

My brother drives the Honda on its last ragged breaths a half hour back to Mount Storm with the windows down, trying to counter the pervasive smell of gas. It's hard to speak with the wind and muffler mingling. I stare down at the passenger door, its plastic inner shell removed. I can see all wires and levers that allow it to open.

We stop at Habitat for Humanity, where my brother negotiates the price of file cabinets with a woman who jokes as if she knows him. He lugs the cabinets outside and puts all his weight into bending their hulking forms into impossible contortions within the smoking car. Customers in the parking lot watch as he pounds on the metal fruitlessly. My suggestions hang like the click of his cowboy boots in the air. Disheveled hair catches in the hinges of his sunglasses. I pull his grocery bags full of pulp-clouded lemonade and raspberry Toaster Strudels into my lap before the metal can crush them.

Nothing is impossible. The file cabinets come home with us, hanging out the trunk. Drawers ebb open and closed with the movement of the road.

We spend the day sweeping nuts and bolts. We untangle wires. He fits things I both do and don't recognize in the neat, rusted drawers. We pull laundry—now all men's—and rewashed food containers from the mass of tangled tools and scrap materials, out of loose pipes that scatter the floor as if the house has blown its arteries. We set pickle jars on piled furniture, sort junk into junk. My brother says he's been working on this on his own. He's been *cleaning out*. We grew up hearing those same words on both sides of the family—our father's father burning mildewed couch cushions and once-great deals in his backyard barrel; visits with our mother's mother marked by gifts in garbage bags, sorted from St. Vincent's and spare rooms that tunneled somewhere through her house's second story.

I sort and sweep the chaos with a deep need to see the wood planks I remember, the syrup of stain pooled in the cracks.

My mother recounts the number of times she has driven down to do the same thing, this *cleaning*. She tells me my brother is stronger than anyone knows. How, when our fragment of the family moved and he insisted on staying home, he woke up in the house every day, nineteen years old and thousands of miles away, breathing cold air inside rooms without electricity all winter.

My old bedroom is his storage room: packed with splintered plastic tubs, yellowed lamps missing bulbs, photo albums that hold the years I remember least with the edges curled. My red-brick dollhouse—painted by my mother's hands—is long gone. Burned by my brother's hands, along with the living room furniture that succumbed to mold.

On my first visit back after more than a year away, I find my succulents and air plants still sitting in red Solo cups on my windowsill. He hasn't touched them. By some miracle, they've stayed where I left them—not a drop of new water while the whole world moved on—and they're still alive.

Acknowledgments

"Overscrambled" was first published by *RUBY.*

"I Stopped Dreaming" was first published by *Writing By Writers (WxW).*

Found text appears on the following pages in this collection:

Page 10—"It Takes a Community To Make a Candle" is from Homesick's "Our Story" (https://homesick.com/pages/our-story)

Page 10—"West Virginia Candle" is from Homesick's West Virginia Candle description (https://homesick.com/products/west-virginia-candle)

Page 32—"Why Do Sliced Apples Turn Brown?" is from Melissa Petruzzelo on *Brittanica* (https://www.britannica.com/story/why-do-sliced-apples-turn-brown)

Page 33—"Unwrapping the Terry's Chocolate Apple" is from Francesca Taylor on Borthwick Institute's blog (http://borthwickinstitute.blogspot.com/2013/09/unwrapping-terrys-chocolate-apple.html)

Page 36—"Rosehip and Apple Jelly" is from Morso Vegan's blog (https://demuths.co.uk/our-blog/article/rosehip-and-apple-jelly)

Page 38—"Rare Old Apples that Taste like Roses" is from a post by Jacqueline & Joseph on Local Harvest's message board (https://www.localharvest.org/blog/25441/entry/rare_old_apples_that_taste)

Page 48—The definition of "musk" is from *Merriam-Webster* (https://www.merriam-webster.com/dictionary/musk)

Page 52—"President: Father Time, Treasurer: Death and Taxes, Secretary: Geo Experience" is from the *Wikipedia* entry for Heluva Good! (https://en.wikipedia.org/wiki/Heluva_Good!)

Page 65—The definition of "salt" is from *Merriam-Webster* (https://www.merriam-webster.com/dictionary/salt)

Page 71—"Place crackers into freezer Ziploc baggie. Crush with rolling pin until they're a coarse crumb" is from *Joy In Every Season*'s "Cracker Crumb Chicken Tenders" recipe (https://www.joyineveryseason.com/main-dishes/cracker-crumb-chicken-tenders/)

SOPHIE HALL writes about homes and fears, especially where the two overlap. Her poems and essays have appeared in *Passengers*, *Yalobusha Review*, *Nat. Brut*, and *RUBY*, among others. She grew up in West Virginia and currently lives in Washington. These days, Sophie is most dedicated to her dream journal. Find her on Instagram @sophieuhmanda or online at sophiehallwriter.com.

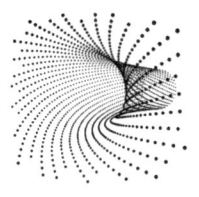

FIRSTMATTERPRESS
Portland, Ore.

Founded in 2018 to dissolve publication barriers for
first-time publishing poets and genre-expanding writers.

2024
FEATURED COVER ARTIST ALEXANDRA STRENFEL

GREENHOUSE
sophie hall

SUSPENDED IN MY INSECTICIDE JAR
clara mcauley

2023
FEATURED COVER ARTIST LARA ROUSE

FLOATING BONES
rae diamond

TEN-CENT FLOWER & OTHER TERRITORIES
charity e. yoro

OUR FAVORITE PEOPLE IN THE ROOM
edited by ash good, lauren paredes & emily moon

2022
FEATURED COVER ARTIST RACHEL MULDER

BETWEEN THESE BORDERS WANDERS A GOLEM
ahuva s. zaslavsky

EVEN THE AIR, TOO HEAVY
riley danvers

ONE ROW AFTER / BIR SIRA SONRA
sonya wohletz

SOMEONE I CAN HOLD GENTLY
xylophone mykland

STORIES FOR WHEN THE WOLVES ARRIVE
hailey spencer

We are a non-profit writer collective press & our authors maintain 100% of book sale proceeds. Please support independent booksellers by purchasing our titles at Bookshop.org

FIRSTMATTERPRESS.ORG

www.ingramcontent.com/pod-product-compliance
Lightning Source LLC
Chambersburg PA
CBHW051640120626
46551CB00014B/2161